FACILITATING TRADE IN VACCINES AND ESSENTIAL MEDICAL SUPPLIES

GUIDANCE NOTE

MARCH 2022

ASIAN DEVELOPMENT BANK

Creative Commons Attribution 3.0 IGO license (CC BY 3.0 IGO)

© 2022 Asian Development Bank
6 ADB Avenue, Mandaluyong City, 1550 Metro Manila, Philippines
Tel +63 2 8632 4444; Fax +63 2 8636 2444
www.adb.org

Some rights reserved. Published in 2022.

ISBN 978-92-9269-383-1 (print), 978-92-9269-384-8 (electronic), 978-92-9269-385-5 (ebook)
Publication Stock No. TIM220048-2
DOI: http://dx.doi.org/10.22617/TIM220048-2

The views expressed in this publication are those of the authors and do not necessarily reflect the views and policies of the Asian Development Bank (ADB) or its Board of Governors or the governments they represent.

ADB does not guarantee the accuracy of the data included in this publication and accepts no responsibility for any consequence of their use. The mention of specific companies or products of manufacturers does not imply that they are endorsed or recommended by ADB in preference to others of a similar nature that are not mentioned.

By making any designation of or reference to a particular territory or geographic area, or by using the term "country" in this document, ADB does not intend to make any judgments as to the legal or other status of any territory or area.

This work is available under the Creative Commons Attribution 3.0 IGO license (CC BY 3.0 IGO) https://creativecommons.org/licenses/by/3.0/igo/. By using the content of this publication, you agree to be bound by the terms of this license. For attribution, translations, adaptations, and permissions, please read the provisions and terms of use at https://www.adb.org/terms-use#openaccess.

This CC license does not apply to non-ADB copyright materials in this publication. If the material is attributed to another source, please contact the copyright owner or publisher of that source for permission to reproduce it. ADB cannot be held liable for any claims that arise as a result of your use of the material.

Please contact pubsmarketing@adb.org if you have questions or comments with respect to content, or if you wish to obtain copyright permission for your intended use that does not fall within these terms, or for permission to use the ADB logo.

Corrigenda to ADB publications may be found at http://www.adb.org/publications/corrigenda.

Notes:
In this publication, "$" refers to United States dollar.

On the cover: (*Clockwise from left*) Employees at the Lugar Research Center in Georgia prepare biological materials in the PCR testing machine purchased through an ADB grant (photo by Tengo Giorbelidze/ADB). Vaccine doses are unloaded from a cargo plane at Phnom Penh International Airport in Cambodia (photo by Chor Sokunthea/ADB). A health worker in the Philippines prepares to extract a dose of vaccine from a vial (photo by Ariel Javellana/ADB). Vaccines arrive in Cambodia through the COVID-19 Vaccines Global Access Facility or COVAX (photo by Chor Sokunthea/ADB). Timely and equitable access to vaccines is key to ending the COVID-19 pandemic (photo by Ariel Javellana/ADB).

Contents

Tables, Figures, and Boxes … iv

Abbreviations … v

1 The Guidance Note: ADB Context … 1

2 Ensure Effective Manufacturing Supply Chains and Equal Vaccine Distribution … 4

3 Guarantee the Efficient Flow of Vaccines and Medical Goods across Borders … 13

4 Funding Modalities for Trade Facilitation and Regional Public Goods … 25

Appendix … 30

Tables, Figures, and Boxes

Tables

1	Process of Vaccine Production, Distribution, and Administration	3
2	Overview of Potential Solutions for Supply Chain Constraints, Efficient Cross-Border Flows	15
3	Epidemic System Preparedness at Points of Entry—A Checklist	15
A.1	Harmonized System Classification for Selected Vaccine-Related Inputs	32
A.2	State of Adoption of United Nations Model Laws and Agreements in the Association of Southeast Asian Nations	33
A.3	Index of Primary References	36

Figures

1	The Complex Journey of a Vaccine	6
2	Top Exporters of Items Needed in Vaccine Production, Distribution, and Administration	7
3	Global Trade Networks of Vaccines and Cold Storage Products, 2019	9
4	Vaccine Manufacturing Requires Extensive Collaboration	10
5	Measure of Preparedness for Cold Chain Logistics in Asian and Pacific Economies	11
6	Flows and Principal Components of Vaccine Cold Chain	20
7	Coronavirus Disease Measures and Funding	27
A.1	Average Number of Nontechnical Measures per Product in the Organisation for Economic Co-operation and Development Countries	31
A.2	Interagency Coordination at the Country Level	34
A.3	E-Learning on Importation and Customs Processes	35

Boxes

A.1	ADB's Trade and Supply Chain Finance Program Contributions to Combat the Pandemic	30
A.2	Legislative Reform to Enable Electronic Transferrable Records in Asia	35

Abbreviations

ACT	Access to COVID-19 Tools
ADB	Asian Development Bank
CAREC	Central Asia Regional Economic Cooperation
COVAX	COVID-19 Vaccines Global Access Facility
DMC	developing member country
ESCAP	Economic and Social Commission for Asia and the Pacific
ICAO	International Civil Aviation Organization
OECD	Organisation for Economic Co-operation and Development
PBL	policy-based lending
RBL	results-based lending
RCI	regional cooperation and integration
RPG	regional public good
SMEs	small and medium-sized enterprises
UNICEF	United Nations Children's Fund
WCO	World Customs Organization
WHO	World Health Organization
WTO	World Trade Organization

Nepal COVID-19 vaccination drive. Elderly persons in the line to receive the Covishield vaccine on 7 March 2021 at a hospital funded by the Republic of Korea in Nepal (photo by Narendra Shretha/ADB).

1 The Guidance Note: ADB Context

The Asian Development Bank (ADB) accords strategic importance to regional cooperation and integration (RCI) to combat the coronavirus disease (COVID-19) pandemic. ADB's Strategy 2030 Operational Plan for Priority 7 indicates that RCI operations need to expand global and regional trade and investment opportunities and increase and diversify regional public goods (RPGs). The guidance note shows the critical nexus between the operational plan's mandates on trade facilitation and RPGs and adds to the broader and growing ADB trade facilitation agenda by focusing on vaccines and medical supplies.[1]

COVID-19 will likely be a warning of future pandemics and disasters unless significant new investments and reforms bolster global, regional, and national preparedness.[2] The manufacturing, distribution, and administration of COVID-19 vaccines and related diagnostics, therapeutics, and medical technologies (medical goods)[3] present

---

[1] According to the Organisation for Economic Co-operation and Development (OECD), trade facilitation covers the full spectrum of border procedures, from the electronic exchange of data about a shipment, to the simplification and harmonization of trade documents, to the possibility to appeal administrative decisions by border agencies. See OECD. Why Trade Facilitation Matters in Today's Global Economy. The scope of trade facilitation includes institutional arrangements and regional and subregional agreements. It is "the simplification, standardization and harmonization of procedures and associated information flows required to move goods from seller to buyer and to make payment" (United Nations Centre for Trade Facilitation and Electronic Business. Trade Facilitation—Principles and Benefits).
[2] See G20. 2021. High Level Independent Panel Urges the G20 to Launch a "Global Deal" to Prevent Catastrophic Costs of Future Pandemics.
[3] Diagnostics (e.g., test kits); therapeutics (e.g., antiviral medicine); and medical technologies (e.g., ventilators).

unprecedented challenges. One effective means of tackling the crisis is to provide timely, accurate information to support national and supranational responses. To speed up sharing of emerging knowledge and best practices to repel the new virus, ADB sponsored the Policy Actions for COVID-19 Economic Recovery (PACER) Dialogues in 2020.

The guidance note offers information and insights on the global pandemic, focusing on trade facilitation and representing a snapshot in time, based on global knowledge shared in documents and online meetings. ADB's Regional Cooperation and Integration Thematic Group may update the guidance note as the pandemic evolves, numbers change, and more knowledge emerges to guide ADB's operations departments and the wider RCI community.

Objectives. The guidance note aims to build a shared framework to understand trade facilitation and border health in the context of the COVID-19 pandemic.[4] The checklist (Table 3) and guiding questions can drive consultations and the policy dialogue with developing member country (DMC) stakeholders organized by ADB staff who identify, commission, undertake or review trade facilitation and RPG interventions to combat current and future pandemics.[5] While trade is a private sector-driven commercial activity, border health and the movement of people and goods across borders are RPGs such as tackling climate change and preserving the environment.

Structure of the guidance note. Coping with the ramped-up production and distribution of vaccines and related medical goods for Asia's 4.6 billion people requires (i) ensuring effective manufacturing supply chains of raw materials for vaccine production: active ingredients and commodities such as glassware; (ii) ensuring equal vaccine distribution; and (iii) guaranteeing the seamless cross-border flow of vaccines and related medical goods. The guidance note presents supply chain and country-specific cross-border flow in two sections for analytical reasons.

Given the unprecedented scale of COVID-19-related trade activities, section II highlights the significance of supply chains for vaccines and essential medical goods, which became more complicated than anticipated. Section III presents information on the what, who, and how of vaccines and related medical goods' cross-border trade and offers solutions to border choke points. Efficient cross-border vaccine flows depend on information technology (IT)-augmented emergency plans and procedures, physical infrastructure investments, and organizational solutions based on specific country needs and aligned to the country's level of readiness. Section IV presents a case for funding modalities that encourage policy reforms and tailor-made investments based on country diagnostics, supply chain analysis, digital transformation–readiness assessments, and country disaster preparedness analysis.

The beginning of each section provides an overview of the key points. Guiding questions at the end of each section explore topics in greater depth, serve as checklists for better results, and lead to action. Boxes, figures, and tables help visualize specific information. An index of primary references listing tools, mechanisms, and essential links is in the Appendix (Table A.3).

---

[4] Border health is a broad term that is characterized by the health care markets, regulatory environments, health laws, environmental factors and health care consumer and individual behaviors (risk and protective) that shape the health of immigrant and other populations living in the region intersected by the geopolitical boundaries of two or more nations (M. L. Zúñiga. 2015. Border Health. New York, NY: Springer).
[5] The guiding questions may be handed out along with ADB's RCI Community subregional and country-specific questions.

Table 1: Process of Vaccine Production, Distribution, and Administration

Drug discovery and development process	Mass production	Distribution and administration	Reverse logistics
• Drug discovery • Preclinical trials • Clinical trials • Approval by regulators	• Selection of suppliers • Ingredient and reagent sourcing • Quality checking • Drug manufacturing • Primary packaging (vials, rubber stoppers)	• Secondary packaging (cold chain equipment) • Warehousing (own or outsourced) • Transport (including last mile) • Storage (freezers) and administration (syringes and vials)	• Returned cold chain equipment (packaging and transport containers)

Source: Organisation for Economic Co-operation and Development. 2021. *Using Trade to Fight COVID-19: Manufacturing and Distributing Vaccines.*

Why are COVID-19 vaccines different?

- Much higher volumes and new target populations
- Multiple products available
- Shifting supply and/or demand dynamics

Handover ceremony. Workers move boxes loaded with COVID-19 vaccines at a handover ceremony on 2 March 2021 at Phnom Penh International Airport, Cambodia (photo by Chor Sokunthea/ADB).

2 Ensure Effective Manufacturing Supply Chains and Equal Vaccine Distribution

"All countries need vaccines, but not all can produce them."

— *Organisation for Economic Co-operation and Development*

Key Points

- Multilateral policy coordination is required to organize vaccine input supply chains.
- Subsidies are crucial to incentivize firms to expand vaccine input production capacity and research and development.
- Vaccine developers and medical goods manufacturers are ramping up their output to provide the quantity and quality needed to combat the pandemic.
- Trade facilitation is essential given the diverse locations of input producers and vaccine manufacturers.
- The unequal distribution of vaccines (as of July 2021) is partly a result of production site locations, financial capacity, and political decisions.
- COVID-19 vaccine and medical goods supply chains have become vastly more complicated than leaders projected because of competing demand, ultracold chain requirements, and politics.
- Medical and technical innovations and innovative health-related infrastructure and supply chain mechanisms are needed to sustain the response to the pandemic and strengthen responsiveness to future threats.
- Limited access to vaccines and related medical goods is the result of supply chain strains and disruptions.
- While the latest estimated vaccine supply may allow immunizing 75% of the global population, public attention is turning to in-country delivery of vaccines and related medical goods: public health supply chain management generally and constraints at the border specifically.
- Country diagnostics are vital as countries' logistics and supply chain management capacities vary hugely across Asia and the Pacific.
- Detailed supply chain assessments using available tools are a precondition for any targeted upgrading efforts.

By 17 September 2021, 5.88 billion COVID-19 vaccine doses had been administered worldwide. While 42.9% of the global population has received at least one dose, only 2.1% of people in low-income countries had received at least a first vaccine as of 22 September 2021.[6] The United States (US) government's work in organizing and subsidizing a complex supply chain for manufacturing COVID-19 vaccines has been lauded as best practice and highlights the importance of government.[7]

Figure 1 presents the different steps of vaccine manufacturing. Each step can be performed in various sites in other countries. Quality control (testing) is essential at each stage and involves the manufacturer and the exporting and importing countries.

The World Trade Organization (WTO) Joint Indicative List of Critical COVID-19 Vaccine Inputs is based on information from pharmaceutical and customs experts, demonstrating the wide range of raw materials, chemical ingredients, and capital equipment needed. ADB's Trade and Supply Chain Finance Program developed a widely

---

[6] Our World in Data. Coronavirus (COVID-19) Vaccinations (accessed 23 September 2021). The UNDP Dashboard for Vaccine Equity figure is slightly higher, see footnote 15.

[7] When building a house, the general contractor is there to ensure the right inputs are available in enough supply at the right time. The electrician cannot install the wiring before the floors, beams, and rough construction are in place. On the other hand, if the sheet rock has already gone up, the plumber cannot install the pipes. Sometimes, the general contractor will move an extra plumber or electrician off one job so that a different job does not fall behind. At its best, the (US administration's national program to accelerate the development, manufacturing, and distribution of COVID-19 vaccines and medical goods) was the general contractor the Americans used to help scale up investments in its entire domestic vaccine manufacturing supply chain (C. P. Bown and T. J. Bollyky. 2021. Here's How to Get Billions of COVID-19 Vaccine Doses to the World. Washington, DC: Peterson Institute for International Economics).

Figure 1: The Complex Journey of a Vaccine

R&D = research and development.
Source: International Federation of Pharmaceutical Manufacturers & Associations. 2019. *Securing Supply through Shared Understanding.*

used web-based supply chain mapping tool early in the pandemic. The tool maps vital medical products, enabling governments, banks, investors, health care professionals, and companies to trace every component in products such as masks or portable ventilators, down to the metal and rubber that goes into each part (Appendix, Box A.1).

The goods required to produce, distribute, and administer vaccines are highly interdependent. Besides the active ingredients needed to manufacture vaccines (input supply chain), vaccine distribution and administration (output supply chain) require access to goods and services created across various countries (Figure 2).[8] The geographical concentration of production[9] and the globally dispersed sources of vaccine ingredients and consumables[10] underscore the importance of trade facilitation, transparent and efficient supply chains, and supply chain integrity.[11]

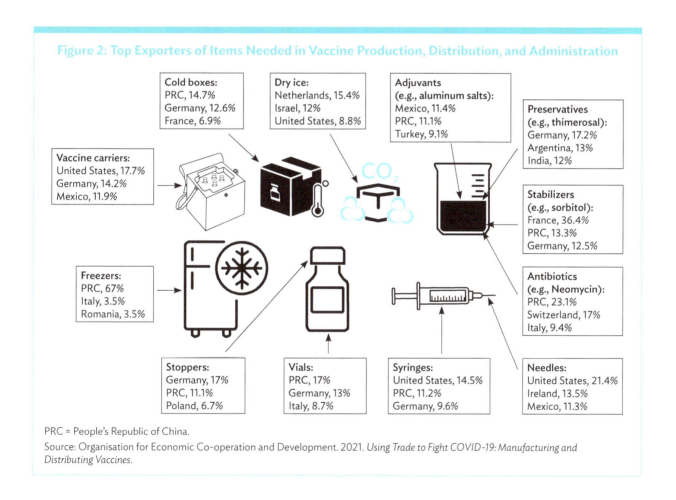

Figure 2: Top Exporters of Items Needed in Vaccine Production, Distribution, and Administration

PRC = People's Republic of China.
Source: Organisation for Economic Co-operation and Development. 2021. *Using Trade to Fight COVID-19: Manufacturing and Distributing Vaccines.*

---

[8] See ADB. Supply Chain Maps for Pandemic-Fighting Products. See also the results of a related WTO technical symposium held on 29 June 2021.
[9] The top 10 exporters account for 93% of global export value and 80% of global export volume. OECD. 2021. *Using Trade to Fight COVID-19: Manufacturing and Distributing Vaccines.*
[10] Consumables such as personal protection equipment.
[11] Aspects of supply chain integrity are procurement mechanisms aligned with current processes, skills, and infrastructure or the lack thereof; measures to curb and combat corruption and overinflated prices; suppliers providing ongoing training as part of their contract; and rigorous and efficient monitoring and recording of supply and stock throughout the supply chain.

The continued pandemic and the increasing demand for vaccines have focused attention on ramping up production.[12] The current increase in vaccine supply[13] will undoubtedly stress output supply chains and border-crossing points as shipments multiply.[14] However, the inequitable access to vaccines remains severe. Six countries, led by the European Union and the US, hold an estimated 90% of the likely surplus of vaccines, which amounts to more than 2.6 billion doses. In contrast, just 3.07% of people in low-income countries had received at least one dose of a COVID-19 vaccine as of 22 September 2021.[15]

While the total available supply may be enough to vaccinate 75% of the global population, the International Association of Pharmaceutical Manufacturers & Associations (IPFMA) voiced its concern that "COVID-19 vaccines currently are not equally reaching all priority populations worldwide."[16] IPFMA came up with a five-step plan on sharing doses, optimizing production, eliminating trade barriers, supporting country readiness, and other innovations to improve vaccine equity.[17] IPFMA calls for the following:

- "Identify trade barriers for critical input materials and support Coalition for Epidemic Preparedness Innovations' (CEPI's) effort to create an independent platform that would identify and address gaps in these inputs and facilitate voluntary matchmaking for fill and finish capacity through the newly established COVID-19 Vaccines Global Access Facility (COVAX) Supply Chain and Manufacturing Task Force;[18]

- "Urge governments, in coordination with the World Trade Organization (WTO), to eliminate all trade and regulatory barriers to export and to adopt policies that facilitate and expedite the cross-border supply of key raw materials, essential manufacturing materials, vaccines along with the prioritized movement of skilled workforce needed for COVID-19 vaccine manufacturing (footnote 17)."

Governments and organizations have implemented a series of trade facilitation measures and actions in response to the COVID-19 pandemic. As information has become abundant and is frequently changing, WTO created the COVID-19 Trade Facilitation Resource Repository (accessed 25 August 2021) to raise awareness and understanding of such actions. Maintaining the flow of safe international trade has emerged as a critical policy tool to confront the challenges of input and output supply chains of urgently needed vaccines and medical goods.

Figure 3 illustrates the global trade network of vaccines and cold storage products that existed before the pandemic. But COVID-19 vaccine and medical goods supply chains have turned out to be vastly more complicated than leaders projected because of competing demands, ultracold chain requirements, and politics. Another reason is the cross-sector innovations required to respond to the pandemic: medical and technical innovations[19] and innovative health-related infrastructure and supply chain mechanisms.

---

[12] Against the backdrop of rising infection rates in Southeast Asia and other countries in mid-July 2021, 17.2 billion vaccine doses had been secured globally. By the end of 2021, the production of COVID-19 vaccines could reach about 11.1 billion doses globally—10 billion doses are required to vaccinate 75% of the world's population aged 5 years and above.
[13] See United Nations Children's Fund (UNICEF). COVID-19 Market Dashboard (accessed 15 July 2021).
[14] Although most low- and middle-income countries (LMICs) are receiving COVID-19 vaccines more slowly than high-income countries, shipments to LMICs have taken place within 12 weeks of introduction in the first high-income countries. The COVID-19 Vaccines Global Access Facility (COVAX) provided essential support.
[15] Global Dashboard for Vaccine Equity. The World in Data figure is slightly lower, see footnote 6.
[16] World Health Organization (WHO). 2021. International Association of Pharmaceutical Manufacturers and Associations.
[17] T. B. Cueni. 2021. *Ensuring the Delivery of Vaccines in Record Time*. 16 June.
[18] COVAX aims to expedite the development and manufacture of COVID-19 vaccines, and to guarantee fair and equitable access for every country in the world. COVAX is the vaccines pillar of the ACT Accelerator, co-led by the Global Alliance for Vaccines and Immunisation (Gavi), the Coalition for Epidemic Preparedness Innovations, and WHO.
[19] Technical innovations include hands-free door openers that can be 3D-printed and basic ventilators. Vaccines using messenger ribonucleic acid (mRNA) and deoxyribonucleic acid (DNA) technology are medical innovations that offer huge advantages over traditional types of vaccines.

Figure 3: Global Trade Networks of Vaccines and Cold Storage Products, 2019

A. **HS 300220 Vaccines** (for human medicine)

B. **HS 901890 Vaccine Carriers** (medical, surgical, or dental instruments not elsewhere classified)

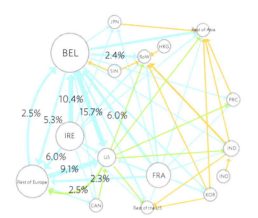
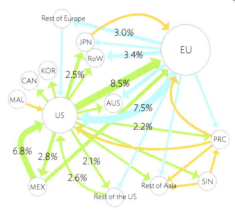

ADB = Asian Development Bank; AUS = Australia; BEL = Belgium; CAN = Canada; EU = European Union; FRA = France; HKG = Hong Kong, China; HS = Harmonized System; IND = India; INO = Indonesia; IRE = Ireland; JPN = Japan; KOR = Republic of Korea; MAL = Malaysia; MEX = Mexico; PRC = People's Republic of China; RoW = rest of the world; SIN = Singapore; US = United States.

Notes: The size of the nodes represents the economy's total export of the commodity group. The thickness of the lines represents the value of the flow of goods between economies. Some lines show the share of exports in the total global exports of the commodity group. For clarity, only exports with high values are represented by the lines. Harmonized System is an international nomenclature developed by the World Customs Organization, which is arranged in six-digit codes allowing all participating economies to classify traded goods on a common basis. Beyond the six-digit level, economies are free to introduce national distinctions for tariffs and many other purposes. (World Trade Organization.)

Source: Asian Development Bank calculations using data from United Nations. Commodity Trade Database (accessed 25 November 2020); and ADB. 2021. Getting Ready for the COVID-19 Roll-Out. *ADB Briefs*. 166. February.

The entire COVID-19 global supply chain needs better organization to accommodate new products and shifts in demand. Firms need subsidies as an incentive to invest in expanding input production capacity. Trade needs facilitation given the diverse locations of producers and manufacturers. And the various stages of manufacturing between vaccine origination and distribution depend on collaboration (Figure 4).

While global attention has focused on input and output vaccine supply challenges, much less time and resources have been dedicated to cross-border and in-country delivery of vaccines, which are potential bottlenecks as supply ramps up. In-country vaccine delivery systems need to be coordinated with domestic demand-side initiatives.

Even though logistics costs are reportedly less than 1% of total vaccination costs, supply chain management and logistics are decisive in the cross-border movement of vaccines and medical goods. The successful COVID-19 response demonstrated that supply chains could meet not only unprecedented ultracold chain requirements of –70°C but also be operational three times faster than the typical 18-month pre-COVID-19 timeline for vaccine distribution.[20]

---

[20] Deutsche Post DHL Group. 2021. Revisiting Pandemic Resilience. *White Paper*. Bonn, Germany.

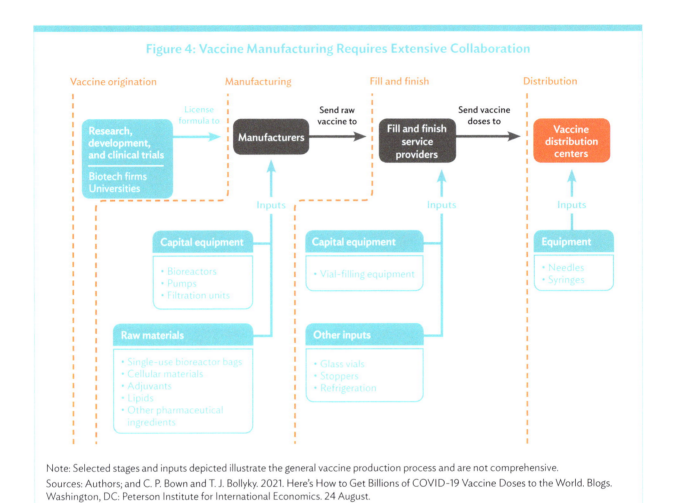

Note: Selected stages and inputs depicted illustrate the general vaccine production process and are not comprehensive.
Sources: Authors; and C. P. Bown and T. J. Bollyky. 2021. Here's How to Get Billions of COVID-19 Vaccine Doses to the World. Blogs. Washington, DC: Peterson Institute for International Economics. 24 August.

Preparedness to cope with logistics challenges varies in economies across the Asia and Pacific region (Figure 5). The United Nations Children's Fund (UNICEF) compiled an overview of seven supply chain assessment tools used in 2018 and 2019 to promote national supply chain capacity investments in medicines and health products.[21] The Access to COVID-19 Tools (ACT) Accelerator[22] and its partners have developed tools for country diagnostics and planning public health supply chains in low- and middle-income countries.[23]

---

[21] UNICEF. 2020. *Technical Review of Public Health Supply Chain Assessment Tools. An Analysis of Major Tools and Approaches 2019.* Copenhagen, Denmark.
[22] The ACT Accelerator is a ground-breaking global collaboration to accelerate the development, production, and equitable access to COVID-19 tests, treatments, and vaccines.
[23] See WHO. COVID-19 Supply Portal (accessed 17 January 2022).

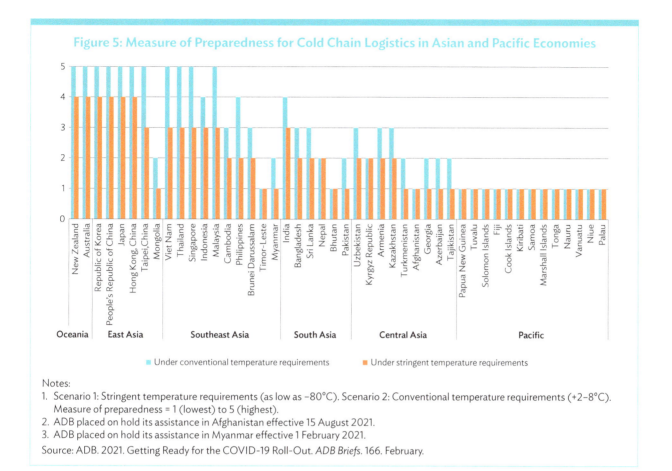

Figure 5: Measure of Preparedness for Cold Chain Logistics in Asian and Pacific Economies

Notes:
1. Scenario 1: Stringent temperature requirements (as low as −80°C). Scenario 2: Conventional temperature requirements (+2–8°C). Measure of preparedness = 1 (lowest) to 5 (highest).
2. ADB placed on hold its assistance in Afghanistan effective 15 August 2021.
3. ADB placed on hold its assistance in Myanmar effective 1 February 2021.

Source: ADB. 2021. Getting Ready for the COVID-19 Roll-Out. *ADB Briefs*. 166. February.

Guiding Questions

❖ **Public sector stakeholders**

- To what degree are national trade facilitation units aware of the current conditions for vaccine input trade frequently involving more than 100 components?
- Are customs and other border agencies prepared to handle the surge of vaccine inputs and vaccine doses?
- Are there any national customs classification issues for vaccine inputs using the WTO Harmonized System categories?
- Have the World Customs Organization (WCO) and the International Civil Aviation Organization (ICAO) streamlined customs procedures to facilitate customs clearance of vaccine inputs?
- How did the public sector support trade facilitation and border health during previous public health emergencies?
- What country diagnostics and assessments do current or did past supply chain investment decisions use?
- Has the potential impact of COVID-19 trade interventions on the trade in non-COVID-19 essential health products been considered?
- Have mandatory safeguard requirements for supply chain integrity been developed and applied?

❖ **Private sector stakeholders**

- Is there a shortage of COVID-19 vaccine inputs manufactured in developing member countries (DMCs)?
- What does it take to incentivize investment to expand the capacity to produce such inputs and ship more supplies to manufacturers' sites?
- Is there a shortage of drivers to transport vaccine inputs because many road transport companies are small and medium-sized enterprises (SMEs) struggling to survive the pandemic?
- How can SME transport operators be kept in business with public support?

❖ **Public and private stakeholders**

- What COVID-19–related supply chain bottlenecks have emerged so far in specific countries?
- Have cyberattacks attempted to block input supplies?
- What specific trade facilitation and logistics interventions have been supported by ADB's Asia Pacific Vaccine Access facility and COVID-19 Pandemic Response Option?
- How can vaccine supply and logistics systems be improved with innovations and investments?
- How can transparency and information sharing across the entire value chain be improved?
- What trade facilitation and logistical support are needed to rapidly scale up the vaccine and medical goods delivery and distribution in specific countries?
- How can demand and supply forecasting and inventory management of raw materials and critical consumables be improved, and by whom?
- Who provides and monitors data on supply chains and export restrictions in specific countries?
- Has investing between pandemics been considered to ensure that systems and industry can sustain their capacity and preparedness?
- What support has been provided by development partners?
- Who has consulted with the government on supply chain assessment tools of choice, considering factors such as available budget, qualified personnel, and time required for assessments?
- What kind of intervention can help raise awareness and tackle the challenge of managing complex international supply chains, frequently involving more than 100 components (upstream) and multiple public and private actors (downstream)?
- Who can mobilize support from the highest political level for trade facilitation and logistics reforms? Is it a role for resident missions?
- How can the ADB partnership with WCO be extended to benefit from knowledge on supply chains and influence customs administrations?
- Should ADB organize knowledge-sharing events in DMCs and for DMCs in cooperation with WCO to share expertise, experience in the region, and good international practices on trade facilitation and logistics to move vaccines and essential supplies?

Sinovac COVID-19 vaccine. Cambodian health staff load CoronaVac doses manufactured by Sinovac of the People's Republic of China on to a refrigerated truck on 17 April 2021 at Phnom Penh International Airport (photo by Chor Sokunthea/ADB).

3 Guarantee the Efficient Flow of Vaccines and Medical Goods across Borders

"Delivery of vaccines depends on supply chains' efficiency."

— *Organisation for Economic Co-operation and Development*

Key Points

- Once the global supply of vaccines matches demand, inefficient cross-border flows will remain a significant obstacle for many countries accessing COVID-19 vaccines and related goods.
- Pacific countries face different distance and cost barriers to vaccine supply.
- Potential solutions to choke points at the border have so far been applied only to a limited extent.
- A better understanding of the what, who, and how of vaccines and medical goods moving across borders is crucial.
- Making permanent what has worked well at the borders during the pandemic and maintaining a state of preparedness are critical to deal with future health threats.

- A national supply management framework for efficient cross-border flows may include (i) an emergency response plan, (ii) IT-enabled supply chain tools for greater transparency and enabling of less intrusive trade inspections, (iii) physical logistics infrastructure, and (iv) organizational solutions for improved coordination and collaboration.
- The emergency response plan unites multiple stakeholders behind the objective of efficient cross-border measures that reduce time and transaction costs, prevent corrupt practices, protect societies from counterfeit products, curb trafficking, and allow information to be shared freely.
- The emergency response plan needs to outline the selected national organizational strategy, its mandate and members, authority, and scope of action.
- Establishing a standardized core unit (interagency coordination committee, emergency operation center, national task force) with broad authority over all trade-related aspects of vaccine and medical goods importation and distribution is paramount.
- The core unit may integrate up to 40 government and private stakeholder groups and thus resemble a national single window.
- Most countries use a technological solution for IT-enabled supply chain transparency. But paper-based data transfer stubbornly remains a widespread form of inefficiency and risk.
- IT investments need to be tailored to the IT readiness status and legislative arrangements of a country to allow a globally harmonized, digitized trade environment.
- Building a cold chain and other storage infrastructure is critical for handling the vast number of vaccine doses and medical goods that began to flow this year and will increase in the coming 2 years.
- Air cargo and land transport capacity will remain vital, and countries need to increase it substantially to reduce constraints on smooth "lab to jab" delivery.
- COVID-19 often requires coordinated responses in days, not weeks and months.
- Effective in-country coordination and regional and global cooperation and partnerships are vital to managing vaccines and medical goods.

Manufacturers predict they can supply 10–11 billion vaccine doses by the end of 2021, 42.8 billion in 2022, and 44.1 billion in 2023.[24] These figures show that manufacturers are optimistic about solving any remaining input supply chain issues with the help of governments if needed. But inefficient cross-border flows remain a big obstacle for countries to access COVID-19 vaccines and related goods.

The urgency and international logistical challenges may have eased since the World Health Organization (WHO) sounded its Public Health Emergency of International Concern alarm on 30 January 2020. But because of the sensitive nature of vaccines, therapeutics, pharmaceuticals, diagnostics, and other medical devices needed to combat the pandemic, any chokepoint that delays them at border crossings can be punishing. In the worst case, essential vaccines and medical goods might expire, causing financial loss and setbacks to national vaccination campaigns that depend on timely delivery. Table 2 raises the alarm.

Solving supply chain issues and sometimes opaque import clearance procedures can avoid chokepoints at the border. Exact information about the involved actors (a plethora of government agencies, including police and security, various commercial actors, and other parties) is as crucial as knowing a country's standard procedures and coordination mechanisms relevant to importing essential medical goods. Epidemic preparedness includes physical and nonphysical investments. The checklist in Table 3 explores the epidemic preparedness of both.

---

[24] For forecast data, see UNICEF. COVID-19 Vaccine Market Dashboard (accessed 12 July 2021).

Table 2: Overview of Potential Solutions for Supply Chain Constraints, Efficient Cross-Border Flows

		Not Exhaustive	Short Term	Medium Term	Long Term	
Enabler	Efficient cross-border flows and regulations	Reconsider export restrictions	XXXXX			🟡
		Build a public stockpile of essential goods	XXXXX			🟡
		Establish mechanisms among stakeholders to monitor and optimize inputs and capacity	XXXXXXXXX			🟡
		Explore risk-based data and testing requirements	XXXXXXXXXX			🟡
		Consider streamlined regulatory mechanisms and tools	XXXXXXXXXX			🟡
		Strengthen mutual regulatory collaboration and collective review		XXXXXXXXX		🟡
		Consider harmonization of requirements			XXXXX	🟡

Note: Observed adoption: ● Widespread ● Partial 🟡 Limited
Source: Adapted from Coalition for Epidemic Preparedness Innovations. 2021. *Towards Vaccinating the World Landscape of Current COVID-19 Supply Chain and Manufacturing Capacity, Potential Challenges, Initial Responses, and Possible "Solution Space."* March. Oslo, Norway.

Table 3: Epidemic System Preparedness at Points of Entry—A Checklist

Areas of Preparedness		Questions
General questions related to border-crossing points	1	Which specific customs entry points allow importing medicines and medical goods?
	2	Are there temperature-regulated storage spaces at each crossing point (cold room at the airport and reefer container plug-in at the seaport)?
	3	Are there functional customs bonded warehouses near airports and seaports?
	4	Do these customs bonded warehouses offer temperature-regulated facilities for the storage of medicines and medical equipment?
	5	Which borders must be crossed in landlocked countries to import medicines and medical equipment? (Indicate specific customs entry and exit points.)
	6	Are there through-transport arrangements at the land border to avoid trans-loading?

continued on next page

Table 3 *continued*

Areas of Preparedness		Questions
Import of COVID-19–related vaccines and medical goods	7	Has the government declared a national essential list of COVID-19 priority items?
	8	Has the regulator in charge approved these priority items to allow their import? Is a specific certification needed from the national drug regulatory authorities?
	9	Has the required administrative order been issued? What is the fast-track procedure for obtaining it?
	10	Has the customs administration defined national extended Harmonized System codes (based on the WCO suggested list) for these items?
	11	Has the list been exempted from preclearance restrictions by all government regulatory authorities?
	12	Which COVID-19–related medicines and medical equipment are prohibited? Which are restricted?
	13	Are there any national guidelines that assist humanitarian actors in importing and delivering medicines and medical equipment (e.g., guidelines for the expiry date of goods from the arrival date, appropriate languages for instructions for use, packaging restrictions, etc.)?
	14	Are vaccines and related medical goods exempt from all import duties, including customs duties, value-added tax, and other taxes and duties?
	15	Alternatively, can the importer deposit duties before the arrival of the shipments (along with the filing of customs declaration)? Or can the importer rely on an undertaker for the release of goods and duties collection?
	16	Is there a provision for duty-free temporary import admission of such shipments to allow, e.g., transport, storage, distribution, or administering of vaccines?
	17	Have airport or land port dues (handling charges, etc.) for the vaccine consignments or collection of fees through an imprest been waived?
	18	Have the administrative focal points for receiving shipping documents in advance been identified, and has this information been shared with importers?
	19	Can the import declaration be filed, processed, and approved electronically for clearance before the shipment's arrival?
	20	What are the expedited and quick-release customs processes for temperature-sensitive medicines and medical equipment?
	21	What are the obstacles related to fast-track customs clearance for future customs audits?
	22	What are the consequences and penalties for failure to account for or regularize importation requirements for essential COVID-19 items?
	23	Have official procedures and standard operating procedures been published and shared with all actors?
	24	Have the customs risk management systems been adjusted to waive physical inspections or tests of vaccines and sensitive medical goods?
	25	Is there a 24/7 clearance service at selected border-crossing points?
	26	For efficient movement of goods across land borders, is there free passage for vehicles carrying vaccines (through-movement) without the need to trans-load them?
	27	Are commercial samples admitted duty-free?

continued on next page

Table 3 *continued*

Areas of Preparedness		Questions
National coordination	28	Does the country use a national single window approach for cross-agency coordination? What is needed to complete the national single window system?
	29	What other agencies and actors are involved in the end-to-end importation process?
	30	Who is the focal point if there is an interministerial task force or coordination body (including customs administration) to expedite the quick release of relief cargo?
	31	Are there preparatory workshops for building capacity and awareness for government agencies and private stakeholders involved in the clearance of vaccines and medical goods?
	32	Is the country using the global resources of the WCO Regional Intelligence Liaison Office and Customs Enforcement Network to deal with illicit or counterfeit trade? Have intelligence and police agencies been involved on both sides of the border to deal with these risks?
	33	If the country has an authorized economic operators (AEOs) program, where is the list of AEOs? Can the approval of AEO status for an importer be expedited?
	34	Does the government maintain a database of sources and authorized importers of vaccines and medical supplies?

Source: Adapted from World Trade Organization. 2021. *Indicative List of Trade-Related Bottlenecks and Trade Facilitating Measures.*

About

15,000 flights

200,000 movements by pallet shippers

15 million deliveries in cooling boxes would be required

10 billion doses under the stringent and conventional scenario

Managing immunization logistics and the vaccine supply chain at the scale demanded by COVID-19 presented an unprecedented challenge. UNICEF's seven supply chain assessment tools highlight opportunities for harmonization and alignment across tools and performance indicators in its technical review.[25] Properly designed cold chain management policies and procedures are essential. The safe handling of vaccines by well-trained personnel and strict adherence to technical requirements and guidelines are equally important.

Making permanent what worked well at the borders during the current pandemic and maintaining a state of continued preparedness are critical lessons learned from the COVID-19 challenge. Transparent cross-border movement of essential medical supplies is a good practice that has emerged in some countries in response to the pandemic. Countries that allowed for efficient entry of goods reduced the wastage of vaccines at borders and improved vaccination outcomes.

[25] UNICEF. 2020. Technical Review of Public Health Supply Chain Assessment Tools. An Analysis of Major Tools and Approaches 2019.

The four cornerstones for a national supply chain management framework consist of (i) an emergency response plan, (ii) IT-enabled supply chain tools for greater transparency, (iii) physical logistics infrastructure, and (iv) organizational solutions.[26] All cornerstones include trade facilitation measures.

National vaccine deployment plans or emergency response plans are valuable for uniting public and private stakeholders behind the objective of efficiently moving health products. Many standards and regulations apply to pharmaceutical products and organic chemicals needed to combat the pandemic, potentially delaying clearance at border-crossing points (Appendix, Figure A.1).

Emergency response plan

➲ **Demand identification.** Define critical product categories and set up demand monitoring and a forecast model.
➲ **Sourcing.** Predefine long and short lists of suppliers for medical supply and logistics services.
➲ **Procurement.** Build up safety stock and secure supply at pre-negotiated prices in advance.
➲ **Inbound logistics.** Select a logistics provider in advance based on capabilities.
➲ **Allocation.** Establish an efficient collaboration model and allocation principle.

The standards and regulations reflect national health risk assessments and conceptions of how business should relate to its stakeholders (consumers, suppliers, etc.). Thus, differing national standards are not superior or inferior to others. Using WCO's Harmonized System[27] approach for all required products and product categories reduces the time needed for nontechnical measures at the border.[28] A list of certified suppliers and experienced logistics providers for medical supplies is vital to avoid delays, avert uncertainty for suppliers and service providers, and reduce the potential for corruption.[29] Agreed cooperation mechanisms among regulators and industry associations are essential to protect societies from counterfeit and substandard medical products. WCO conducted a series of webinars in early 2021, supported by vaccine manufacturers, to better equip customs agencies to identify fake products and curb trafficking. Any emergency response plan should include real-time information sharing among stakeholders for more speed, efficiency, and reduced transaction costs.

Well-known technological solutions to facilitate trade include automation of business processes, digital uploads of supporting documents, use of risk management, prearrival processing, postclearance audit, authorized economic operator program, national single window,[30] e-payments, use of nonintrusive inspection equipment, and advance exchange of electronic data. Despite enormous achievements,[31] paper-based transferable data remain a form of inefficiency and risk in international trade. Because of the ongoing pandemic, "many would have expected to see a groundswell in the adoption of technology platforms offering paperless trade services. Yet anecdotal evidence suggests that uptake in the existing providers has been lackluster, with percentage use in the single digits."[32]

---

[26] Adapted from Deutsche Post DHL Group. 2020. DHL White Paper—Delivering Pandemic Resilience. September.
[27] WTO has initiated a project to identify the critical COVID-19 vaccine inputs, including their tariff codes.
[28] Appendix, Table A.1 provides an example of selected Harmonized System classified vaccine inputs.
[29] See UNICEF's supply division services.
[30] A Single Window is a paradigm of governance in which traditional government regulatory functions are re-engineered into transparent, efficient and predictable services to meet the needs and expectations of citizens and businesses (adapted from World Trade Organization. 2021. Indicative List of Trade-Related Bottlenecks and Trade-Facilitating Measures on Critical Products to Combat COVID-19).
[31] We have seen 10 years of digital innovation in roughly three months and e-commerce across the globe has increased by two to five times from the levels prior to the pandemic (McKinsey & Co. 2021. The Eight Trends that Will Define 2021 and Beyond. June).
[32] ADB and International Chamber of Commerce. 2021. *Digitizing Trade in Asia Needs Legislative Reform*. Manila.

Digital technology has, therefore, been key in ADB's COVID-19 response, e.g., e-customs systems, electronic cargo tracking systems, intelligent transport systems, and digital health records. Every significant IT investment should include measures against cybersecurity attacks.

Information Technology-enabled supply chain transparency

- **Data sharing.** Adapt existing IT solutions to set up a logistics data-sharing platform.
- **Data collection.** Reinforce timely, accurate and standardized data collection.

Governments across the world are at different phases of their digital transformation.[33] Each country needs a plan based on its needs, aligned to its state of readiness.[34] The World Bank's Digital Government Readiness Assessment toolkit is a comprehensive diagnostic tool to help governments assess their status of digital transformation.[35] ADB has published a *Digital Health Implementation Guide for the Pacific*.[36] Digitizing trade in Asia needs legislative reform and global standards and protocols to drive interoperability. ADB's Trade and Supply Chain Finance Program works with the International Chamber of Commerce and the Government of Singapore to establish a globally harmonized, digitized trade environment, which includes the expedited adoption of United Nations (UN) model laws and agreements in the Association of Southeast Asian Nations (ASEAN) region.[37] According to OECD (2021, p. 12), "Improving transparency and information sharing across the entire supply chain will enable the different actors to find each other and enable more efficient distribution via trade channels."[38]

To handle 10 billion doses of vaccine by the end of 2021 presents a formidable challenge. **Physical infrastructure** is a core element of any supply chain management framework. Just-in-time or direct shipping models are not always suited to serve many vaccination points or countries with largely remote populations. And up to 70% of health facilities in low- and middle-income countries cannot store large volumes of COVID-19 vaccines at 2°C–8°C or –20°C and colder (Figure 6).

Physical logistics infrastructure

- **National safety stock.** Build up national safety stock and ensure efficient stock cycling.
- **Logistics infrastructure.** Predetermine logistics partners, supply routes, and transport modes under different scenarios.

---

[33] Several governments will claim having automated their customs systems while detailed analysis may reveal the abundant use of paper-based work. Often, basic technical tools such as electronic scanners to inspect containers are not available or computers are not kept under appropriate external conditions (temperature, dust).

[34] The technically most advanced solution to efficiently operate highly complex and "unstable" logistics systems and supply chains (e.g., for vaccines) uses Internet of Things (IOT) technology, which requires converting telemetry-generated networks of sensors across long distances from a reactive rule-based model to a predictive model. Such a model avoids unplanned stoppages and delays and solves problems before they become critical. The number of logistics and medical experts and engineers is insufficient to read the vast amounts of telemetry that will be generated by IoT delivering 10 billion doses of vaccines in less than 12 months. Artificial intelligence technology that allows experts to transfer their knowledge to computers and replicate it or decentralize it for simultaneous application across the logistics network is the solution. It would provide the ability to replicate and leverage the decisioning performance of experts throughout the vaccine network and system to manage outcomes and adjust their models to changing needs. The "virtual experts" have vastly increased capacity and can be integrated and deployed anywhere and in any operational environment. See Analycat. Using Sue AI for COVID-19 Vaccine Logistics.

[35] World Bank. 2020. Digital Government Readiness Assessment (DGRA) Toolkit V.3 1, Guidelines for Task Teams (Version 3.0). April.

[36] ADB. 2021. *Digital Health Implementation Guide for the Pacific*. Manila.

[37] Appendix, Table A.2 displays the low adoption rates of UN model laws and agreements.

[38] OECD. 2021. *Using Trade to Fight COVID-19: Manufacturing and Distributing Vaccines*.

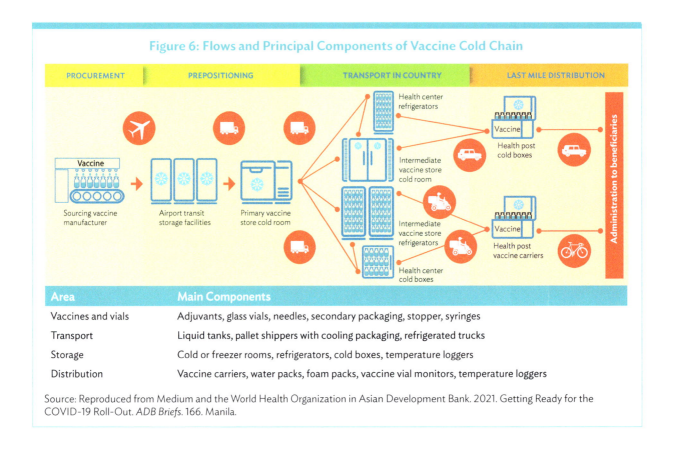

Figure 6: Flows and Principal Components of Vaccine Cold Chain

Area	Main Components
Vaccines and vials	Adjuvants, glass vials, needles, secondary packaging, stopper, syringes
Transport	Liquid tanks, pallet shippers with cooling packaging, refrigerated trucks
Storage	Cold or freezer rooms, refrigerators, cold boxes, temperature loggers
Distribution	Vaccine carriers, water packs, foam packs, vaccine vial monitors, temperature loggers

Source: Reproduced from Medium and the World Health Organization in Asian Development Bank. 2021. Getting Ready for the COVID-19 Roll-Out. *ADB Briefs*. 166. Manila.

Governments must explore setting up appropriate storage infrastructure at border-crossing points, considering the time, cost, and utilization of large-scale cold chain storage and warehousing.

National safety stock and logistics infrastructure are essential for epidemic preparedness. This includes (i) maintaining, depending on the setting, robust subnational, national, or regional stockpiles of medical supplies and emergency supply chain mechanisms; (ii) establishing routine capabilities and effective public health responses at points of entry to ensure border health; and (iii) conducting regular emergency simulations and other cross-sector preparedness activities. An emerging lesson is that funding for epidemic preparedness requires upfront investment in physical infrastructure to close the gaps.

Closed airports and lack of flights can be additional bottlenecks because air cargo supply chains are critical to pandemic response efforts worldwide. Even though the number of cargo flights that operated globally in 2020 expanded by 2.74% in 2020,[39] year-over-year, passenger aircraft belly cargo capacity—usually amounting to about 45% of overall air cargo—became severely constricted because of the steep decline in overall flights.[40] Quarantine constraints on air cargo flight crews aggravate the shortage of cargo space.[41] Military flight support has helped in some cases to deliver vaccines and testing equipment. Seamless movement of vehicles for overland

---

[39] See ICAO. 2021. *Air Transport Monthly Monitor*. April.
[40] When the world reached 3 million confirmed COVID-19 cases in April 2020, global international passenger capacity declined by an estimated and unprecedented 94% in the same month. ICAO. 2021. *Effects of Novel Coronavirus (COVID-19) on Civil Aviation: Economic Impact Analysis* (accessed 10 October 2021).
[41] The International Air Transport Association (IATA) estimates that global passenger air traffic will be back to normal only in 2025.

transport, where applicable, has its issues. Cross-border traffic suffers from quarantine regulations for drivers and the various infrastructure constraints that make the "lab to jab" route bumpy. In addition, according to Jens Hügel, senior adviser at the International Road Transport Union, "80% of the firms engaged in distribution and logistics of vaccines and medical goods are SMEs, and many of these companies are in a challenging financial situation."[42]

Organizational solutions are the fourth cornerstone of a practical supply chain management framework. They are an essential element of the emergency response plan. Given the complexity and challenges associated with the efficient flow of medical supplies across borders, countries have benefited from developing nerve centers or task forces to set a singular strategy and manage activities. Such a consultative or coordination mechanism can quickly spot, communicate, and deal with technical barriers to trade and end-to-end supply chain concerns. Existing public–private consultation structures such as national trade facilitation committees[43] can manage specific logistics and border challenges. WHO called for joint incident management team meetings across the region at the onset of the pandemic. WHO generally suggests an interagency coordination committee[44] as an effective national core unit. Another option is to take a command center approach to drive extensive collaboration. Successful emergency operations centers, such as the one developed in Nigeria to combat polio[45] represent global good practice.

Institutionalized core unit
- **Task force.** Preestablish a task force with authority, agility, and credibility
- **Organization.** Capture key organizational elements in the emergency response plan

Whatever organizational approach a country chooses to ensure speedy and secure evacuation of vaccines and essential medical goods at the border, advocacy and proactive stakeholder education on the need for wider-scale coordination of national responses are vital for interdisciplinary and multisector actions.[46] And one agency must be nominated to handle the entire clearance process and deliver shipments after their clearance.

Any institutionalized core unit for the effective deployment of vaccines and all related activities and processes needs to include public and private sector representatives across functional areas and jurisdictions (medical, logistics, regulatory). Cooperation and coordination are warranted among private sector actors. For instance, airport operators and ground handlers must be as prepared as freight forwarders and airlines to deal with essential medical goods' volume and specificity.

Health security is a regional public good in Asia and the Pacific, where the movement of goods, services, business travelers, and labor across borders is constant. Asia's subregional cooperation platforms represent an effective transnational organization model that has facilitated collective responses to the COVID-19 pandemic.

---

[42] International Road Transport Union and World Trade Organization. 2021. *Proceedings of the COVID-19 Vaccine Supply Chain and Regulatory Transparency Technical Symposium.* 29 June 2021. Manila.
[43] OECD. 2021. *Using Trade to Fight COVID-19: Manufacturing and Distributing Vaccines.*
[44] See Appendix, Figure A.2.
[45] McKinsey & Company. 2021. *"None Are Safe until All Are Safe": COVID-19 Vaccine Rollout in Low- and Middle-Income Countries.*
[46] The IMPortation And Customs Clearance Together! (IMPACCT) Working Group, for instance, offers e-learning modules on importation and customs processes (Appendix, Figure A.3).

- Since the pandemic began, Central Asia Regional Economic Cooperation Program (CAREC) members have jointly responded to the crisis. They have strengthened information sharing on COVID-19 responses and practices among CAREC countries, established the CAREC Working Group for Health, and formulated the CAREC Health Strategy 2030 (for endorsement in November 2021).

- The South Asian Association of Regional Cooperation agreed on a joint response plan for South Asia that includes a COVID-19 emergency fund. Health and trade officials adopted a telemedicine framework, collaborative diagnostics, and therapeutic research and agreed on pragmatic solutions to promote trade.

- The Greater Mekong Subregion (GMS) agreed on the COVID-19 Response and Recovery Plan 2021–2023, protocols on infectious diseases, and the GMS Health Cooperation Strategic Framework, underscoring health security as a regional public good.

The rapid spread of COVID-19 showed that a multicountry organizational approach is needed, and responses must include contributions from sectors other than health, notably trade and logistics. Existing international disease response coordination mechanisms such as the Asia Pacific Strategy for Emerging Diseases and Public Health Emergencies, the Global Health Security Agenda, and International Health Regulations require additional multicountry and multisector efforts to tackle the pandemic.

Guiding Questions

- **Public sector stakeholders**

  - Which trade facilitation measures helped streamline border processes for pharmaceutical and medical goods during the pandemic emergency? (For example, green lanes or corridors for fast clearance, electronic submission of simplified documents for pre-arrival processing, agreed lists of Harmonized System codes coordinated with WHO, nonintrusive clearance process, classification of air cargo crews and truck drivers as essential workers, and extended business hours at specific border posts.)
  - Which of these measures was made permanent, which was not, and why?
  - Has more efficient testing at the border sped up identifying health threats?
  - What efforts have been made to streamline regulatory mechanisms and tools?
  - Is what constitutes essential medical goods in the COVID-19 context completely visible?
  - Are essential medical goods stockpiled?
  - Do any tariffs on medicines, vaccines, and essential medical equipment restrict imports?
  - Does the country have a national emergency response plan?
  - Does the national emergency response plan include (i) improved regulation on risk-based data, testing requirements, and harmonized requirements for vaccine manufacturing and/or essential products; (ii) monitoring of vaccine delivery and distribution to maintain product integrity and reduce wastage; and (iii) better compliance based on transparent regulations and penalties and accompanied by adequate supervision and oversight for better enforcement?
  - Have government standard procedures and coordinating mechanisms for importing essential medical goods been shared with all relevant public and private stakeholders?

- Are there country-level cold chain guidelines that describe proper storage methods and temperatures, offer temperature-monitoring practices, and recommend steps for maintaining and evaluating temperature controls?
- How well have countries identified the extended WCO Harmonized System codes for all essential medical goods?
- Is the government promoting IT-enabled supply chain transparency improvements such as (i) replacing the remaining paperless trade measures with IT solutions to speed up the clearance and avoid potential contagion from paper-based documentation such as rubber stamping and signatures on documents; and (ii) open access to relevant data as a precondition for successful cooperation between the private and the public sectors?
- Does the government consider adopting the UN Model Law on Electronic Transferable Records, which aims to create a harmonized, digitized trade environment?
- Has the government embarked on renewing, expediting, or completing the national and regional single window integration of manual and automated processes?
- What is the degree of interagency cooperation among customs and other agencies to streamline processes at the border or on sanitary and phytosanitary standards at ports, airports, and border-crossing points?
- Which agency leads the coordination of clearing shipments at the border?
- Are there long-term policy commitments for improving logistics infrastructure, particularly cold chain management and storage infrastructure?
- Is there a subregional or regional vaccine procurement and deployment approach to support national strategic plans and prepare vaccination programs?
- Is the government committed to investing in capacity development as a cross-functional priority? In establishing proper cold chain management practices and developing supply chain managers and a trained workforce to optimize the supply chain system and service its components?[47] In developing customs administrations in cooperation with WCO?
- Does the government take a regional view of logistical hurdles? For instance, does it grant temporary seventh-freedom traffic rights to allow planes to transport freight or passengers between two countries without touching down in their home country?
- Who in the government leads the promotion of interoperability using regional cooperation and coordination mechanisms?
- Is there a coordinated approach to border economic zones or an inclusive health strategy for border populations?

Public and private stakeholders

- Were roundtable meetings used to bring together national and international public and private stakeholders as a first step to establish the collective action needed for effective health sector supply chains?
- Did national consultative coordination mechanisms raise stakeholder awareness about the actions, resources, and procedures required at the border to respond to the pandemic effectively?
- Have air-cargo operators been pre-authorized to fly additional services without restrictions?
- Are there quarantine restrictions for air cargo flight crews?

---

[47] Optimizing supply chains and servicing their components entail demand planning; real-time, end-to-end cold chain temperature shock and moisture monitoring; postvaccination tracking to efficiently plan for second dosage and recurring vaccine applications; limitation of vaccine counterfeiting, tampering, contamination, and theft; and management of last-mile delivery.

- What priority is given to e-customs systems, electronic cargo tracking systems, and corresponding digital and cybersecurity investments?
- Has ICAO's Regional Office Asia Pacific called on national civil aviation authorities concerning a multilateral agreement to temporarily liberalize air cargo services?
- Is there any support for land transport SMEs to help them maintain critical capacity for cross-border road haulage?

❖ **International development partners**

- What interventions support the proactive collaboration mindset needed to integrate up to 40 organizations and their mandates for the single window reform?
- Did subregional programs organize regional policy dialogues on cross-border health risks and encourage regional information sharing and surveillance on health and trade issues?
- Do subregional partners coordinate the exchange of knowledge, information, and best practices to improve vaccine delivery across borders and vaccination rates and reach the common goal of adequate immunization coverage more efficiently and effectively?
- Are there regional procurement initiatives for medical supplies accompanied by fast-track importation and emergency regulatory procedures?
- Is national coordination capacity sufficient to absorb available international cooperation assistance (funding, advocacy, capacity building, and policy advice)?
- Have networks and development partnerships been leveraged at the country level to identify and resolve any emerging choke points in vaccine access and production, including trade and customs clearance issues, regulatory hurdles, financing, and use of private sector logistics networks?
- What kind of support and initiative can incentivize stringent regulatory bodies to work together globally and develop international assessment protocols and quality assessment criteria that DMCs can adopt?

ADB and UNICEF deliver medical equipment to Nepal. A $300,000 grant from ADB to UNICEF funded the purchase of emergency medical supplies and equipment for health workers in support of Nepal's ongoing COVID-19 response (photo by Narendra Shretha/ADB).

4 Funding Modalities for Trade Facilitation and Regional Public Goods

Funds Are as Important as Policy Action to Boost Trade Facilitation

Key Points

- The COVID-19 pandemic has mobilized record amounts of resources for fiscal and monetary support measures.
- International financing institutions, public donors, public–private alliances, and governments have committed funds that may be sufficient to allow vaccination of the global population, although unequal distribution remains a problem.
- As of August 2021, adequate vaccine supply and upfront funding was center stage. Investing in trade facilitation and distribution of vaccines and essential medical goods has attracted less attention.

- Preparing countries for future pandemics, disasters triggered by natural hazards, and climate change effects needs upfront precautionary investments to fill gaps in country preparedness.
- Policy action and a commitment to reform are needed to deal with some critical parameters of the previous two sections, which weigh on the seamless flow of vaccines and medical goods.
- The required policy and trade facilitation reforms make a case for policy-based lending and results-based lending.
- Policy-based lending can tackle domestic and regional policy and regulatory reforms, and results-based lending can finance a share of governments' national emergency and trade facilitation upgrading plans, including reaching out across borders.
- ADB's 2019 Regional Cooperation and Integration Conference encouraged participants to step up involving the private sector, engaging subregional cooperation platforms and associations, and using new financing modalities and instruments.

According to ADB's COVID-19 Policy Database, the pandemic has mobilized record amounts of resources. As of 26 July 2021, the total amount announced by ADB's members to combat the COVID-19 pandemic has amounted to $31.147 trillion, including the $3.775 trillion from ADB's DMCs.[48] Figure 7 summarizes COVID-19 macroeconomic measures and their sources of funding. Five measures correspond to monetary policy (1–4) and fiscal policy (5). "There is a use relationship in measures 1–5 and a funding relationship in measures 6–8, which is the 'double counting' accounting corollary for these measures."[49] International assistance is a source of funds for governments and likely ends up in measure 5.

The total amount of ADB assistance was $20.592 billion as of 16 July 2021 and included regional projects. Most of the international aid pledged are for the purchase of vaccines.[50]

The seamless movement and rollout of vaccines and essential medical supplies are critical for full economic reopening and recovery. Yet, delays in vaccine delivery and rollout are significant. As of March 2021, Asia and the Pacific had administered about 2 doses per 100 people compared with more than 20 per 100 in leading countries such as the United States.[51] Trade-related issues already described constitute a significant challenge for the timely delivery of vaccines and related medical goods.

With the global pandemic in its second year and not abating, upfront financing and precautionary investment can boost trade flows and supply. The guidance note advocates using available multiple-country diagnostic tools before making any investment decisions. Policy action and a commitment to reform are preconditions for dealing with critical trade-related parameters for a successful response to the COVID-19 pandemic. The required policy and trade facilitation reforms establish a case for policy-based lending (PBL) and results-based lending (RBL).

- PBL can handle "software" issues, including domestic policy and regulatory reforms. The accelerated implementation of existing global and regional agreements such as the WTO Trade Facilitation Agreement, the WTO Revised Kyoto Convention, and the UN Economic and Social Commission for

---

[48] ADB. ADB COVID-19 Policy Database (accessed 17 August 2021).
[49] Measures and packages included in the database are mostly intentions and announcements of authorities. Information on actual amounts spent or transacted are not always available. See ADB. Key Responses to COVID-19 by the Asia-Pacific Economies: An Update from the ADB COVID-19 Policy Database (accessed 17 August 2021).
[50] For details see A. D. Usher. 2021. A Beautiful Idea: How COVAX Has Fallen Short. *The Lancet*. 397 (10292). pp. 2322–5.
[51] C. Y. Park, K. Kim, and M. Helble. 2021. Achieving A Better COVID-19 Vaccine Rollout. *Asian Development Blog*. Manila: ADB.

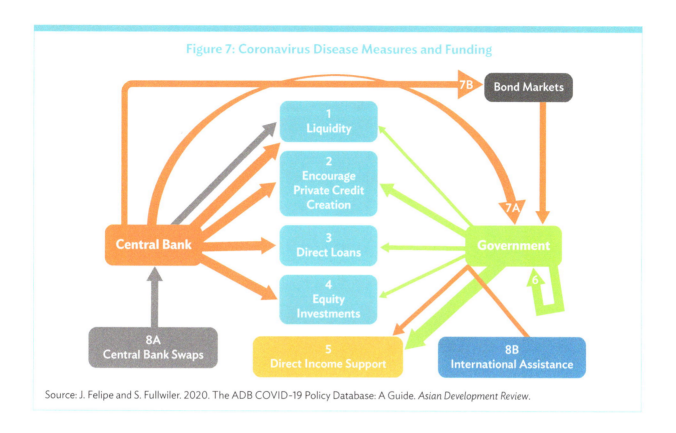

Figure 7: Coronavirus Disease Measures and Funding

Source: J. Felipe and S. Fullwiler. 2020. The ADB COVID-19 Policy Database: A Guide. *Asian Development Review*.

Asia and the Pacific (ESCAP) Paperless Trade Agreement can anchor such lending.[52] PBL can help harmonize policies and regulations with neighboring countries to make cross-border trade more seamless and ease digital trade.

Considering PBLs in the context of cross-border cooperation must overcome the challenges to develop regional results frameworks and align regional members' individual aspirations around a joint strategy. Existing subregional economic cooperation platforms with an agreed strategy and road maps offer advantages for expediting PBL processing.

PBL can help arrange partnerships, which are essential to responding to the COVID-19 crisis. PBLs are successful provided they do not overload partnerships with objectives. Capacity development and analytical work that accompany PBLs are essential. Formal and informal communication platforms are helpful for mobilization and consensus-building (e.g., customs officers' meetings of subregional programs). Subregional partnerships to manage common public health concerns can meet emerging demand for RPGs such as border health to fight the pandemic.

- RBL programs have three features that distinguish them from other lending modalities. They (i) finance a share of the government's investments in national trade facilitation upgrading and emergency

---

[52] The WTO Trade Facilitation Agreement will improve trade efficiency worldwide, encouraging economic growth by cutting red tape at borders, increasing transparency, and taking advantage of new technologies; The revised Kyoto Convention promotes trade facilitation and effective controls through its legal provisions on applying simple yet efficient procedures. The convention is complemented by guidelines, which indicate some possible courses of action in applying standards, transitional standards, and recommended practices, and describe best practices; The ESCAP Paperless Trade Agreement is a UN treaty dedicated to accelerating trade digitalization across the Asia and Pacific region through capacity building, pilot testing, harmonization, and mutual recognition of paperless trade systems.

plans, (ii) rely on government systems and institutions for implementation and risk management, and (iii) disburse funds when intermediate results or results agreed with the borrower and measured by disbursement-linked indicators have been achieved.

Most countries were not prepared for the COVID-19 challenge and had no border immunization programs. Border health was not on the agenda. A successful immunization campaign requires seamless transport across borders, storage and logistics infrastructure, and health facilities; sufficient medical personnel; safety monitoring; and strong public awareness and advocacy campaigns on both sides of the border. The ACT Accelerator and its partners have developed tools for country diagnostics and planning.[53]

Using country diagnostics to design PBL and RBL programs is crucial. The guidance note refers to several diagnostic tools and provides a checklist on pandemic preparedness at border-crossing points in (Table 3). ESCAP, WTO, and WCO offer helpful checklists and guidelines for implementing international agreements.[54] PBL and RBL operations offer four lessons, which can inform the initial consultative stage of processing ADB assistance:[55]

- Allow all public and private actors to align around a new goal or well-defined result.
- Take a longer-term perspective on lending to sustain policy reforms despite possible changes of government.
- Flip the policy dialogue and ask where the government wants to be in 5 years and work backward from there instead of first discussing problems, inputs, and finance.
- Institutionalize results measurement criteria in countries and regions.
- Acknowledge that the process of reaching a consensus is as important as achieving results.

ADB's RCI Conference 2019 encouraged operations departments to become more aspirational[56] when using RBL or PBL for cross-border projects, including RPGs, by

- using single and multicountry PBLs and/or RBLs to create space for the private sector, e.g., to promote commercialization and state-owned enterprise reforms (ports and logistics); harmonize trade regulations, operating standards, and procedures; and encourage the greening of cross-border connectivity (e.g., green ports);
- using regional platforms to systematically create opportunities for sovereign and nonsovereign operations and public–private partnerships;
- using technical assistance for capacity and pipeline development to allow for more inclusive trade; and
- developing financing instruments to accelerate public and private investment in RPG projects.

---

[53] WHO. 2020. COVID-19 Vaccine Introduction Readiness Assessment Tool. 21 September; WHO. 2021. Guidance on Developing a National Deployment and Vaccination Plan for COVID-19 Vaccines. 1 June; WHO. 2021. COVID-19 National Deployment and Vaccination Plan: Submission and Review Process. 29 January.
[54] UNESCAP. Readiness Assessment Guide For Cross-Border Paperless Trade (accessed 8 August 2021); WTO. 2014. Briefing Note: Trade Facilitation—Cutting "Red Tape" at the Border. 12 February; WCO. 2008. Revised Kyoto Convention. Guidelines. 17 April.
[55] ADB RCI Conference 2019: Proceedings. Session VI: The Rationale and Potential for Results- and Policy-Based RCI Operations. 27–28 November 2019. Manila.
[56] ADB. RCI Conference 2019: Post-Conference RCI–Thematic Group Briefing with Directors General. January 2020.

Guiding Questions

- What is the breakdown of national resources mobilized for monetary policies, fiscal measures, and complementing of international assistance to combat the COVID-19 pandemic?
- What are the estimated funds already committed or required to guarantee the seamless move of vaccines and related medical goods at the border?
- Has the government considered increased investments in digital infrastructure (automated tools) essential to strengthen cooperation mechanisms and risk management at borders?
- Have equal investments in data and cybersecurity been considered?
- What country diagnostic tools and checklists have been used or chosen to identify current funding gaps in epidemic preparedness at the border?
- Has the government invested in epidemic surveillance as a critical component of public health practice and border health and sufficient laboratory and minimum research capacities to identify virus variants?
- Have policy actions and a commitment to reform been discussed with governments?
- Which national agency can champion the alignment of all actors around a new goal or well-defined result?
- Does the country have experience with results measurement systems?
- What is the country's positive experience with PBL and RBL for trade facilitation interventions and the generation of RPGs to combat the pandemic?
- What diagnostic tools, lessons from past interventions, and guidelines have steered the design of PBL and RBL interventions?
- Has creating space for private sector investments been considered in the design of sovereign operations?
- Can regional platforms be used to create opportunities for nonsovereign interventions and public–private partnerships to boost trade facilitation and the creation of RPGs?
- What kind of technical assistance is conducive for capacity and pipeline development to promote more inclusive trade?
- What are the estimated time and resources needed in the coming years to improve DMCs' resilience and preparedness to deal with epidemics, disasters triggered by natural hazards, and climate change impacts?

Appendix

BOX A.1

ADB's Trade and Supply Chain Finance Program Contributions to Combat the Pandemic

Early in the coronavirus disease (COVID-19) pandemic, the Trade and Supply Chain Finance Program (TSCFP) came up with a widely used web-based supply chain mapping tool. It maps vital medical products, enabling governments, banks, investors, health-care professionals, and companies to trace every component in products such as masks or portable ventilators, down to the metal and rubber that go into each part.

Small and medium-sized enterprises were hit hard by the pandemic. They are the backbone of the Asian economy, making up more than 96% of enterprises and contributing 42% of gross domestic product. TSCFP's supply chain finance business aims to reduce financing gaps faced by small and medium-sized enterprises to help them become part of the global trading system.

The TSCFP Digital Standards Initiative creates digital standards and protocols to drive interoperability between fintech platforms and components of the trade ecosystem. The TSCFP Anti-Money Laundering Initiative aims to reduce unintended consequences of regulation and to improve detection, investigation, and prosecution of trade-based money laundering. The TSCFP Capacity-Building Initiative includes online courses on trade finance, supply chain finance, and other topics.

Source: Asian Development Bank.

Appendix

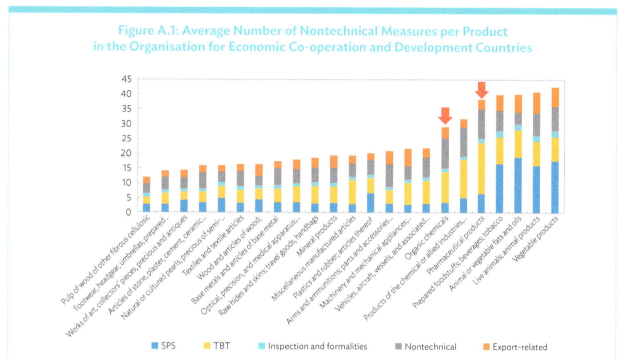

Figure A.1: Average Number of Nontechnical Measures per Product in the Organisation for Economic Co-operation and Development Countries

SPS = sanitary and phytosanitary, TBT = technical barrier to trade.
Source: Organisation for Economic Co-operation and Development. 2021. *Using Trade to Fight COVID-19: Manufacturing and Distributing Vaccines* (accessed 19 July 2021).

Table A.1: Harmonized System Classification for Selected Vaccine-Related Inputs

Category	Product	Short Description	HS Code
Ingredients	Thimerosal	Preservatives – to prevent contamination	285210
	Aluminum salts	Adjuvants – to help stimulate a stronger immune response	283322
	Sorbitol	Stabilizers – to keep the vaccine potent during transportation and storage	290544
	Formaldehyde	Inactivating ingredients – to kill virus or inactive toxins	291211
	Neomycin	Antibiotics – to prevent contamination by bacteria	2941
	Sterols	Lipid nanoparticles in mRNA vaccines	290613
Primary packaging	Vials	Serum bottles, vials, and other phamaceutical containers of glass	701090
	Stoppers	Articles of vulcanized rubber n.e.s., except hard rubber	401699
Secondary packaging: Storage and distribution	Insulated cartons		4819
	Vaccine carriers		901890
	Cold boxes		392310
	Refrigerators or freezer chests		841850
	Freezers		841830
	Dry ice		281121
Secondary packaging: Vaccine administration	Syringes		901831
	Needles		901839

HS = Harmonized System, mRNA = messenger ribonucleic acid, n.e.s. = not elsewhere classified.
Source: Adapted from Annex Table B.1 in Organisation for Economic Co-operation and Development. 2021. *Using Trade to Fight COVID-19: Manufacturing and Distributing Vaccines.*

The Model Law on Electronic Transferable Records, developed by the UN Commission on International Trade Law, holds the promise of increased efficiency, consistency, and coherence in harmonizing legislation in a global and cross-border regulatory environment that could level the playing field for all. Recognition of the model law within the domestic legal systems of trading nations will make it the single most potent driver of electronic record adoption.

Table A.2: State of Adoption of United Nations Model Laws and Agreements in the Association of Southeast Asian Nations

County	MLEC (1996)	MLES (2001)	CUECIC (2005)	CPTA (2016)	MLETR (2017)
ASEAN Countries					
Brunei Darussalam	2000	N/A	N/A	N/A	N/A
Cambodia	2019	N/A	N/A	Signed 2017	N/A
Indonesia	N/A	N/A	N/A	N/A	N/A
Lao PDR	2012	N/A	N/A	N/A	N/A
Malaysia	2006	N/A	N/A	N/A	N/A
Myanmar	N/A	N/A	N/A	N/A	N/A
Philippines	2000	N/A	Signed 2007	Acceded 2019	N/A
Singapore	1998	N/A	Ratified 2010	N/A	2021
Thailand	2019	2001	N/A	N/A	N/A
Viet Nam	2005	2005	N/A	N/A	N/A
CAREC Countries					
Afghanistan	2020	N/A	N/A	N/A	N/A
Azerbaijan	N/A	N/A	Acceded 2018	Acceded 2018	N/A
Georgia	N/A	N/A	N/A	N/A	N/A
Kazakhstan	N/A	N/A	N/A	N/A	N/A
Kyrgyz Republic	N/A	N/A	N/A	N/A	N/A
Mongolia	N/A	N/A	Acceded 2020	N/A	N/A
Pakistan	2002	N/A	N/A	N/A	N/A
People's Republic of China	2004	2004	Signed 2006	Approved 2020	N/A
Tajikistan	N/A	N/A	N/A	N/A	N/A
Turkmenistan	N/A	N/A	N/A	N/A	N/A
Uzbekistan	N/A	N/A	N/A	N/A	N/A
SASEC Countries					
Bangladesh	2006	N/A	N/A	Ratified 2020	N/A
Bhutan	2006		N/A	N/A	N/A
India	2000		N/A	N/A	N/A
Maldives	N/A	N/A	N/A	N/A	N/A
Nepal	N/A	N/A	N/A	N/A	N/A
Sri Lanka	2017	N/A	Ratified 2015	N/A	N/A

ASEAN = Association of Southeast Asian Nations, CAREC = Central Asia Regional Economic Cooperation, CPTA = Framework Agreement on Facilitation of Cross-border Paperless Trade in Asia and the Pacific, CUECIC = United Nations Convention on the Use of Electronic Communications in International Contracts, Lao PDR = Lao People's Democratic Republic, MLEC = 1996 UNCITRAL on Electrionic Commerce, MLES = 2001 UNCITRAL Model Law on Electronic Signatures, MLETR = 2017 UNCITRAL Model Law on Electronic Transferable Records, N/A = not applicable, SASEC = South Asia Subregional Economic Cooperation, UN = United Nations, UNCITRAL = United Nations Commission on International Trade Law.

Notes:
1. Myanmar is also a member of SASEC but is included in the ASEAN section of this table.
2. ADB placed on hold its assistance in Afghanistan effective 15 August 2021.
3. ADB placed on hold its assistance in Myanmar effective 1 February 2021.

Sources: UNCITRAL; Renard et al. 2021. *Digitizing Trade in Asia Needs Legislative Reform*. Manila: Asian Development Bank.

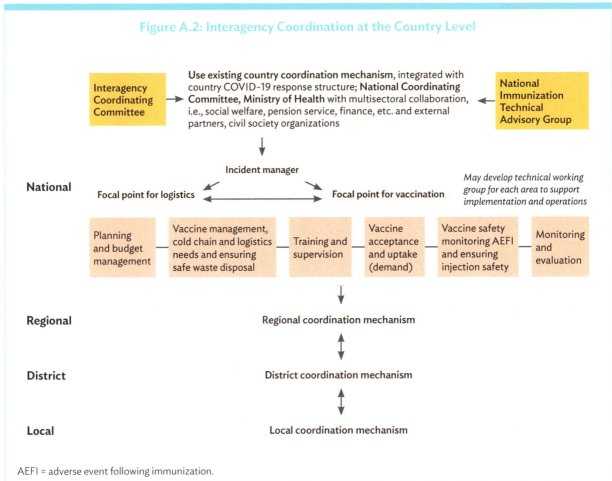

Figure A.2: Interagency Coordination at the Country Level

AEFI = adverse event following immunization.
Source: World Health Organization and United Nations Children's Fund. 2021. *Guidance on Developing a National Deployment and Vaccination Plan for COVID-19 Vaccines, Interim Guide*. Geneva.

Source: Importation and Customs Clearance Together Working Group. Cross-Border Movement of Humanitarian Relief Consignments (accessed 29 July 2021).

BOX A.2

Legislative Reform to Enable Electronic Transferrable Records in Asia

A major roadblock to greater use of paperless trade solutions is the lack of legal recognition of electronic transferable records. The single greatest driver of electronic record adoption in the postpandemic era will be their recognition within the domestic legal systems of trading nations. A solution exists in the form of the Model Law on Electronic Transferable Records, developed by the United Nations Commission on International Trade Law, but adoption of the Model Law on Electronic Transferable Records has been limited to just a few three jurisdictions to date.

In partnership with the International Chamber of Commerce, Enterprise Singapore, and the Asian Development Bank, the International Chamber of Commerce Digital Standards Initiative was launched in 2020. The Digital Standards Initiative is focused on the establishment of a globally harmonized, digitized trade environment. It envisions digital standards that enable seamless digital trade throughout the trade ecosystem, with end-to-end interoperability for exporters, shippers, ports and customs authorities, logistics providers, financiers, and importers. This will translate into enhanced resilience in trade finance and supply chain processes, increased productivity, the introduction of new services at scale, and the advancement of the United Nations Sustainable Development Goals. This initiative will leverage technology to reduce the global trade finance gap, particularly among micro, small, and medium-sized enterprises.

Sources: International Chamber of Commerce; Asian Development Bank.

Table A.3: Index of Primary References

Organization	Subject and Link
Country Diagnostics	
WHO	COVID-19 Vaccine Introduction Readiness Assessment Tool
WHO	COVID-19 National Deployment and Vaccination Plan: Submission and Review Process, 29 January 2021
WHO, UNICEF	Guidance on Developing a National Deployment and Vaccination Plan for COVID-19 Vaccines
Digital Transformation	
World Bank	Digital Government Readiness Assessment (DGRA) Toolkit V.3 1, Guidelines for Task Teams
ADB	Digital Health Implementation Guide for the Pacific
ADB	Legislative Reform to Digitize Trade in Asia
Logistics	
Analycat. Using Sue AI for COVID-19 Vaccine Logistics.	
ICAO	Air Transport Monthly Monitor
Subregional, Regional, and Global Agreements	
UNCITRAL. *UNCITRAL Model Law on Electronic Transferable Records*.	
WTO	Trade Facilitation Agreement
WTO	Revised Kyoto Convention
UN ESCAP	Paperless Trade Agreement
Supply Chain and Trade Facilitation	
WTO	List of Vaccine Inputs
ADB	Supply Chain Maps for Pandemic-Fighting Products
WTO	COVID-19 Trade Facilitation Resource Repository
WHO	COVID-19 Supply Portal
UNICEF	Technical Review of Public Health Supply Chain Assessment Tools: An Analysis of Major Tools and Approaches
WTO	Harmonized Systems
WTO	National Single Window
IMPACCT	E-Learning on Importation and Customs Processes
Vaccine Supply	
UNICEF	COVID-19 Market Dashboard
Our World in Data	Coronavirus (COVID-19) Vaccinations
United National Development Programme, WHO	Global Dashboard for Vaccine Equity
ADB	COVID-19 Policy Database
ADB	Asian Development Blog
The Lancet	A. D. Usher. 2021. A Beautiful Idea: How COVAX Has Fallen Short. *The Lancet*. 397 (10292). 19 June. pp. 2322–5.

ADB = Asian Development Bank, ICAO = International Civil Aviation Organization, IMPACCT = IMPortation And Customs Clearance Together!, UN ESCAP = United Nations Economic and Social Commission for Asia and the Pacific, UNICEF = United Nations Children's Fund, WHO = World Health Organization, WTO = World Trade Organization.

Source: Asian Development Bank.